We Are All People

A Children's Book About Tolerance

Written by Lucas A Catton
Illustrated by R Cunningham

ISBN 978-0-578-55240-8

We are all born out of love, the destiny of humankind.

Some brown, some white, some black, some red and any others you might find!

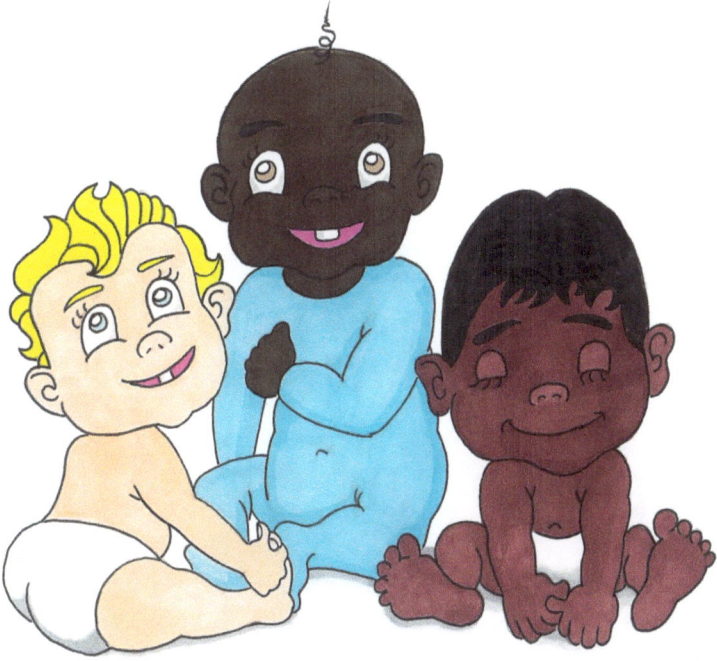

We don't choose when or where we're born, or get to choose our DNA.

Some are born into different faiths, and that is perfectly okay!

We may look different on the outside, but inside we're all the same.

Because we are all people, playing one big game!

We all need things like food, water, shelter and protection.

Everyone deserves respect and connection!

We may not talk the same or walk the same, or even eat or wear the same things.

But we can learn so much from each other and rejoice in what everyone brings.

Notice how many people you come in contact with each day.

They are all unique
and perfect in their
own special way!

The Golden Rule is a beautiful thing, one that serves us well.

So lend a hand, share a smile and cast a wonderful spell!

We all deserve plenty of love, peace and happiness.

Because we are all people, let us celebrate for we are blessed!

Dedication

To Max, Rhett, Ella and all children everywhere. Thank you for breathing life into this beautiful world!